MW00612706

I, II & III John
FOR BEGINNERS

MIKE MAZZALONGO

THE "FOR BEGINNERS" SERIES

The "For Beginners" series of video classes and books provide a non-technical and easy to understand presentation of Bible books and topics that are rich in information and application for the beginner as well as the mature Bible student.

For more information about these books, CDs and DVDs visit: **bibletalk.tv/for-beginners**

ISBN: 978-1-945778-75-9

BibleTalk Books
14998 E. Reno
Choctaw, Oklahoma 73020

Scripture quotations taken from the New American Standard Bible®, Copyright © 1960, 1962, 1963, 1968, 1971, 1972, 1973, 1975, 1977, 1995 by The Lockman Foundation Used by permission. (www.Lockman.org)

TABLE OF CONTENTS

CHAPTER 1
INTRODUCTION

This study will be examining the three epistles written by the Apostle John, who also wrote the Gospel of John and the book of Revelation. Some think that these letters do not have the weight of other more lengthy epistles, but what they lack in length, they make up in substance. John's letters are a tremendous source of apologetic material (defense of the faith) as well as information about true Christian living.

Let us begin by briefly examining the life of their author, the Apostle John.

Background on John

We have a lot of information about John, the writer of these epistles, from different parts of the Bible and other historical sources. Here are 10 facts that summarize John's life and work:

1. He was one of the sons of Zebedee and Salome (Matthew 27:56; Mark 15:40).

2. He was partnered in a fishing business with his brother James and two other brothers, Andrew and Peter, and from this connection was drawn into Jesus' circle of disciples who lived in Capernaum, Jesus' adult home (Matthew 4:13).

3. He was impetuous and zealous. Jesus called John and his brother "sons of thunder" because they

wanted God to destroy a Samaritan village that would not receive the Lord (Luke 9:54; Mark 3:1).

4. John's mother asked Jesus for choice positions in the Kingdom for her sons (Matthew 20:20-23).

5. He sat next to Jesus after he and Peter prepared the room where they ate the Passover meal and where Jesus instituted the Lord's supper (John 13:23 - the Apostle loved by Jesus).

6. He was, along with Peter, the first to see the empty tomb where Jesus had been laid after His crucifixion (John 20:3-5).

7. According to tradition, John made Jerusalem his home until the death of Mary (Jesus' mother) who had been put in his care by the Lord Himself at the cross (John 19:26-27).

8. John later moved to Ephesus which eventually became the geographical and numerical center of Christianity after the destruction of Jerusalem (70 AD).

9. From Ephesus John wrote his gospel, three epistles, and after a period of exile on the island of Patmos, he returned to Ephesus to write his final work, the book of Revelation.

10. He trained many early church leaders like Polycarp, Papias and Ignatius who would eventually write about him and the early church. These historical records have been preserved to this day. John is believed to have lived to an old age and died in Ephesus where he lived and worked for many years.

Background on the Epistle — I John

John's letters deal with the problem of Gnosticism. As Gentiles entered the church in greater numbers, they brought much of their philosophical ideas with them. Gnosticism was an attempt by some in the church to fuse Greek philosophical ideas with Christian theology. This was done in an effort to make the Christian religion more palatable to educated Greeks.

In simple terms, Gnosticism taught that "spirit" was good and "matter" was evil. Salvation, therefore, required one to escape the realm of matter (what was physical) and enter into the realm of spirit. These ideas were connected to the Greek concept of "duality." The Gnostic teachers taught that the way to make this escape or transfer was through "knowledge" (what the word gnosis means). Not any knowledge however, but the special knowledge held in secret by these same Gnostic teachers.

The conflict with the gospel and this teaching came in the form of questions concerning Jesus' identity. The contradiction for the Gnostics was the idea that something good, someone of God, someone who was God, someone who was spirit, came in the form of matter/humanity. Gnostics taught that matter was evil and the way to escape was through either the practice of self-denial or the complete embrace of hedonism (self-gratification). The problem for these teachers was that Jesus, the divine Son of God, came in the form of flesh/matter, practicing neither extreme self-denial nor self-gratification. He was not a self-indulgent sinner, but neither was He an ascetic like John the Baptist.

The Gnostic teachers tried to resolve this problem (that a divine spirit inhabited a physical body - something they believed was impossible) by teaching that the spirit of Christ only entered Jesus at baptism and left Him before He died on the cross (thus the divine spirit was only visiting and not fully part of Jesus' essential being). Another way to realign the gospel with their Greek ideas was to say that Jesus was not really human, He only appeared to be human (thereby preserving the idea that spirit and matter were not compatible since Jesus was only Spirit and simply appeared to be physical). In other words, He was only a spirit appearing in the form of a man. By teaching this they were able to preserve their Greek idea of "dualism" while still acknowledging that Jesus was the Son of God. Their error lay in the fact that they denied the full humanity of Jesus in their description of His nature.

In Ephesus a man named Cerinthus was the leader of this movement and claimed to have special mystic experiences as well as exalted knowledge which could elevate his students. He taught that Jesus was Joseph's physical son and received God's Spirit at baptism but it left Him at the cross. In response to this John writes three epistles (letters) for a church that was facing new philosophies that were threatening to undermine its basic doctrines: that Christ was both fully God and man simultaneously. John's letters were meant to help the church maintain apostolic teaching against the perversion of the first (but not last) doctrinal threat.

The Letter — I John

The first epistle of John is keyed to his personal eyewitness experiences with the living, breathing Jesus, not a pure spirit or apparition. Like the Gospel of John, this letter emphasizes the reality of Jesus but in philosophical terms. John is fighting a false philosophical system that uses imagery and esoteric concepts to explain itself and convince others. He responds by presenting the case for Jesus, an actual living and divine being, in philosophical and conceptual terms (light/love). John takes these abstract ideas and presents them in a practical way so that his readers can fully grasp the concepts given to them by the real Jesus and apply these to their everyday lives. John is not only responding to the false teachers by setting forth correct ideas and teachings, he is also ministering to his flock with words of encouragement about and from their faith.

The heretics' effect on the church was to cause doubt about Jesus' existence as well as their own possibility of salvation through Jesus alone, without the secret knowledge promoted by the Gnostic teachers. These individuals simply wanted spiritual power over the souls of the saints. They were teaching both Christians, as well as those turning to Christ from paganism, that the way to true salvation lay in the path of the secret knowledge that only they possessed. This technique has been used throughout history by various false teachers who insist on adherence to a particular doctrine other than the gospel, or leader other than Christ Himself in order to be saved. We know, however, that the "doctrine" changes and the "leaders" come and go, but the method (a different gospel or a new leader with a vision or secret) is always the same.

John's first epistle emphasizes once and for all that we receive salvation through Jesus Christ alone, and we can be certain of it. After establishing that Jesus was both fully man and fully God, John goes on to explain the three ways that we can be certain of our salvation, and none of them have anything to do with secret knowledge or special teachers. Salvation is both available and attainable for all.

Outline — I John

1. **The Historical Jesus (1:1-4)**

   o   Jesus the real person as seen by John

2. **Certainty by Walking in the Light (1:5-2:29)**

   o   Personal Conduct

   o   Social Relationships

   o   Separation from the World, not Separation from our Bodies

   o   Adherence to Truth

3. **Certainty by Abiding in Love (3:1-4:21)**

   o   Ethical Proof of Love - Good Conduct

   o   Social Proof of Love - Good Deeds

   o   Theological Proof of Love - Faith in Jesus as God

   o   Emotional Proof of Love - No Fear, Love of the Brethren

4. **Certainty by Exercising Faith (5:1-12)**

   o   Not by Secret Knowledge

5. **Conclusion (5:13-21)**

John's gospel tells the story of the transformative power of the cross. John's first epistle encourages his readers to continue believing that particular and freely accessed knowledge. There is no secret knowledge, the truth has been revealed once for all and for everyone to see, that Jesus is the Christ and that everlasting life is through Him and Him only. This knowledge transforms us from lost to saved, condemned to forgiven, sinners to saints, members of the kingdom of darkness to members of the kingdom of light, slave to free, empty to filled with the Holy Spirit, and temporal to eternal.

John's writings tell us that we will one day leave our fleshly body, but the departure will not be produced by secret knowledge. Our transfer to a glorious body will be accomplished through faith in Jesus Christ based on our knowledge of Him freely given to us through the gospel.

Reading Assignment: I John 1:1-2:29

CHAPTER 2
WALKING IN
THE LIGHT

I JOHN 1:1-2:29

In the previous chapter we began the study of I John by reviewing the character and history of John the Apostle and the circumstances in which he wrote this epistle. We will now review the possible reason why this letter was written.

In the first century the main non-Jewish group to enter the church were Greeks. They brought with them many of their former ideas and philosophies which they tried to merge with Christian thought. One of these was the notion that in order to be saved, a person needed certain "special knowledge," knowledge that had the power to transfer an individual from the realm of the physical to the realm of the purely spiritual. Usually these secret instructions involved restrictions about certain food and other types of ascetic practices. These and other ideas were contained in a system of thought referred to as Gnosticism, and the teaching of it caused several problems in the church.

Those promoting these ideas were trying to change the teachings concerning the character of Christ in order to better fit their Greek thought and philosophy. Since the Apostles taught that Jesus was both God and man, the Gnostic teachers had trouble reconciling the idea that a divine being could dwell in a human form. They taught that you were one or the other, but could not be both. Their solution was to claim that Jesus was only a spirit who appeared to be a man. This violated the Apostles' teachings and reduced Jesus to the status of a ghost or an apparition, not the Divine Son of God coming as a man to die for the sins of all and resurrect from the dead to conquer death for all.

Their teaching was meant to control the minds and the lives of their followers, not to free them with the gospel of Christ. Their doctrine also undermined the effect of the gospel by causing Christians to doubt their salvation and eventual resurrection. Believers began to ask themselves the following questions, "If Christ was a ghost, who then died for my sins? Are my sins dealt with by the cross or by my own efforts to learn and apply this secret knowledge? If Christ was an apparition, is there any bodily resurrection for Him or me? If He was a ghost, is that what I will become also, a ghost?"

To counter this dangerous teaching and bolster the sinking faith of the ones affected by it, John writes a letter that has two main objectives:

1. To establish the true identity and character of Jesus.

2. To restore the disciples' confidence in the certainty of their salvation through Christ and Christ alone.

In I John 1:1-2:29 John begins by describing the Jesus that he knew personally and one of the three ways in which they could be certain of their salvation.

The Historical Jesus — 1:1-4

> [1]What was from the beginning, what we have
> heard, what we have seen with our eyes, what we
> have looked at and touched with our hands,
> concerning the Word of Life— [2]and the life was
> manifested, and we have seen and testify and
> proclaim to you the eternal life, which was with the
> Father and was manifested to us— [3]what we have
> seen and heard we proclaim to you also, so that
> you too may have fellowship with us; and indeed
> our fellowship is with the Father, and with His Son
> Jesus Christ. [4]These things we write, so that our
> joy may be made complete.
> - I John 1:1-4

John was an Apostle and the criteria for being an Apostle
was that you had to be an eyewitness of Jesus' life from His
baptism by John the Baptist through to His death, burial and
resurrection (Acts 1:12-26). This means that when he writes
this letter he writes as one who has personally witnessed the
life, death and resurrection as well as the ascension of
Jesus. He writes about what he has witnessed, not
conjecture or opinion. In the end, his readers must choose to
believe what he teaches based on what he has seen, or the
Gnostic teachers' secret wisdom based on their
philosophies.

John does not refer to Jesus by His given name, but by titles
that the Lord has as well as qualities of His nature and
position that the Apostle has used before in his gospel. For
example:

- I John Verse 1 - What was from the beginning (John 1:1)

- I John Verse 1 - Word of Life (John 1:1;4)

- I John Verse 2 - The life (John 1:4)
- I John Verse 2 - The eternal (John 10:28)
- I John Verse 2 - With the Father (John 1:1)
- I John Verse 2 - Manifested to us (John 1:4)

In verse 3 he finally gives the name of the person he has referred to in six other ways in the previous verses. These titles are given and used to establish the divine nature of Jesus Christ. He is at the source of creation and time which begins with creation. He embodies the life-giving Word. He gives life in the sense that He is the life-giving Spirit in human form. He is eternal, with no beginning or end. He is with God. He has been made manifest meaning that His true nature has been divinely revealed. All of these terms can only be applied to a divine spiritual being, thus establishing Jesus as a fully divine spirit.

John also mentions that he knew or experienced Jesus in a very physical way as well:

- Heard Him speak - verse 1
- Saw Him with his eyes - verse 1
- Touched Him with his hands - verse 1

According to John, Jesus was no vision, he was able to interact with Him just like any other human being. As a matter of fact, what Jesus has received from God (as only a divine spirit could receive), He has given to John (as only one person could give to another) and John is passing it along to them in his gospel and in this letter. Of course, what he is passing along is the good news surrounding the death, burial and resurrection of Christ, and the offer of eternal life to every person who believes. This eternal life is seen or described as a fellowship that all believers have together, have with the Apostles, have with Jesus and ultimately with God. He concludes by telling them that the purpose of his letter is to encourage them to remain faithful so that John and the others might rejoice in their faith. There will be no joy for John if they fall away.

Certainty by Walking in the Light — 1:5-2:29

The next section gives the readers a first way that they can be certain of their salvation. Remember, they are struggling with the idea that Jesus may only be an apparition and John has responded by describing his first hand contact with the Lord. They also have begun to doubt if any real change has taken place, if they truly have been saved. They want some kind of evidence that will confirm that they are truly spiritual, truly eternal in nature and thus saved.

John answers by saying that one way they can be certain of the transformation in themselves is to note the difference in their present lifestyle. Again, John uses a figure of speech to convey this idea. For Jews as well Greeks light represented what was true, good, pure and spiritual in nature. Walking in the light meant that one's life reflected these characteristics. It was another term for a "saved person."

In chapters 1 and 2, John names four areas where one's conduct determined if they were truly in fellowship with other Christians, John, the Apostles, Jesus and the Father. He tells them to examine their conduct and if it matches this, they have a guarantee that they are saved, an eternal spirit, and walking in the light.

No time to read and analyze every verse but in essence these are the four areas he talks about.

1. Personal Behavior

[5]This is the message we have heard from Him and announce to you, that God is Light, and in Him there is no darkness at all. [6]If we say that we have fellowship with Him and yet walk in the darkness, we lie and do not practice the truth; [7]but if we walk in the Light as He Himself is in the Light, we have fellowship with one another, and the blood of Jesus His Son cleanses us from all sin. [8]If we say that we have no sin, we are deceiving ourselves and the truth is not in us. [9]If we confess our sins, He is faithful and righteous to forgive us our sins and to cleanse us from all unrighteousness. [10]If we say that we have not sinned, we make Him a liar and His word is not in us.

[1]My little children, I am writing these things to you so that you may not sin. And if anyone sins, we have an Advocate with the Father, Jesus Christ the righteous; [2]and He Himself is the propitiation for our sins; and not for ours only, but also for those of the whole world.

[3]By this we know that we have come to know Him, if we keep His commandments. [4]The one who says, "I have come to know Him," and does not keep His commandments, is a liar, and the truth is not in him; [5]but whoever keeps His word, in him the love of God has truly been perfected. By this we know that we are in Him: [6]the one who says he abides in Him ought himself to walk in the same manner as He walked.
- I John 1:5-2:6

A person who is walking in the light (and thus is a saved person) is a person who recognizes certain things about their personal behavior:

1. That they are sinners, and do not hide or pretend they are not.

2. They do not pretend they are good but secretly practice sin.

3. They confess their sins and seek forgiveness regularly.

4. They understand that without the blood of Christ they cannot be cleansed and walk in the light.

You know you are walking in the light when you recognize that you are a sinner, make an honest effort to abide by God's word, but depend completely on Jesus' blood to keep you clean, worthy and saved.

2. Social Relationships

[7]Beloved, I am not writing a new commandment to you, but an old commandment which you have had from the beginning; the old commandment is the word which you have heard. [8]On the other hand, I am writing a new commandment to you, which is true in Him and in you, because the darkness is passing away and the true Light is already shining. [9]The one who says he is in the Light and yet hates his brother is in the darkness until now. [10]The one who loves his brother abides in the Light and there is no cause for stumbling in him. [11]But the one who hates his brother is in the darkness and walks in the darkness, and does not know where he is going because the darkness has blinded his eyes.

^{12}I am writing to you, little children, because your sins have been forgiven you for His name's sake. ^{13}I am writing to you, fathers, because you know Him who has been from the beginning. I am writing to you, young men, because you have overcome the evil one. I have written to you, children, because you know the Father. ^{14}I have written to you, fathers, because you know Him who has been from the beginning. I have written to you, young men, because you are strong, and the word of God abides in you, and you have overcome the evil one.
- I John 2:7-14

A person who is walking in the light, and thus secure in their salvation, is a person who loves their brother. There is a hierarchy of importance in Jesus' teachings, they are all divine, worthy of respect and obedience but some are weightier than others. Jesus said Himself, "Woe to you, scribes and Pharisees, hypocrites! For you tithe mint and dill and cummin, and have neglected the weightier provisions of the law: justice and mercy and faithfulness; but these are the things you should have done without neglecting the others." (Matthew 23:23).

The Lord placed our attitude towards others, especially those in the body, as of primary importance, and issues surrounding church structure, worship style after. For example, one who worships correctly and has a proper understanding of doctrinal matters but fails to genuinely love his brother fails to walk in the light and will bear the consequences. If you are going to make a mistake, better it be in church matters and issues of the true meaning of difficult passages than the neglect of others or hatred towards the Christian family.

John mentions the young and the old because all are responsible for these things. Young and old, leaders and followers are all responsible and capable by God's Spirit to love. Failing to do so is a reflection of darkness not light. Love is the surest sign of divine light in our lives.

3. Separation from the World

> [15]Do not love the world nor the things in the world. If anyone loves the world, the love of the Father is not in him. [16]For all that is in the world, the lust of the flesh and the lust of the eyes and the boastful pride of life, is not from the Father, but is from the world. [17]The world is passing away, and also its lusts; but the one who does the will of God lives forever.
> - I John 2:15-17

This is a response to that "secret knowledge" that said that entry into a pure spiritual world was achieved by leaving our bodies. According to these teachers, the way to do this was by giving up certain foods, legitimate sex within marriage and other ascetic practices. John says that the proof that one is walking in the light is that a person separates himself from the world, not from his body. The Apostle urges them to give up worldliness (excessive love and preoccupation with physical things, things that simply gratify the senses) by recognizing that this world and all that is in it is temporary and will ultimately be destroyed.

You know you are walking in the light (saved) when your final goal is going to heaven, not making yourself comfortable here.

4. Adherence to Truth

[18]Children, it is the last hour; and just as you heard that antichrist is coming, even now many antichrists have appeared; from this we know that it is the last hour. [19]They went out from us, but they were not really of us; for if they had been of us, they would have remained with us; but they went out, so that it would be shown that they all are not of us. [20] But you have an anointing from the Holy One, and you all know. [21]I have not written to you because you do not know the truth, but because you do know it, and because no lie is of the truth. [22]Who is the liar but the one who denies that Jesus is the Christ? This is the antichrist, the one who denies the Father and the Son. [23]Whoever denies the Son does not have the Father; the one who confesses the Son has the Father also. [24]As for you, let that abide in you which you heard from the beginning. If what you heard from the beginning abides in you, you also will abide in the Son and in the Father.

[25]This is the promise which He Himself made to us: eternal life.

[26]These things I have written to you concerning those who are trying to deceive you. [27]As for you, the anointing which you received from Him abides in you, and you have no need for anyone to teach you; but as His anointing teaches you about all things, and is true and is not a lie, and just as it has taught you, you abide in Him.
[28]Now, little children, abide in Him, so that when He appears, we may have confidence and not shrink away from Him in shame at His coming. [29]If you know that He is righteous, you know that

everyone also who practices righteousness is born of Him.
- I John 2:18-29

Walking in the light is demonstrated by teaching the truth and John states that the truth of God is the fact that Jesus is the Christ and Savior. Jesus, the divine Son of God, came in the flesh. This is the essence of truth, the dividing line between false teachers and teachings, and true teachers and their teachings. He warns them against the many false teachers (calls them antichrists) who will teach something other than this. This is reference to the Gnostic teachers and their doctrines. "Going out from us" means leaving the teachings of the Apostles. The "anointing" is the reception and maintenance of the Holy Spirit who proclaims and maintains the pure gospel.

In the end, John tells them that they have received the truth though the inspired word of the Apostles (calls this the anointed or anointing). They are walking in the light so long as they continue to hold fast to these words and not abandon them for other teachings.

Summary

John gives them four ways to assure themselves that they are walking in the light (saved).

- Their good conduct assures them.

- Their love of others assures them.

- Their focus on heaven assures them.

- Their hold on the gospel assures them.

He finishes by telling them that if they assure themselves in these ways they will be confident and happy when Jesus returns and will not be afraid and ashamed of their conduct. If they know Jesus, they know how to act, and acting in the way He would have them act (these four ways) will make them confident in His presence.

Reading Assignment: I John 2:28-3:24

CHAPTER 3
ABIDING IN LOVE

I JOHN 2:28-3:24

John is writing to Christians who have been influenced by false teachings concerning the identity of Christ and the manner in which they are saved. These Gnostic teachers are proposing the idea that Jesus was only a spirit, and in order to be truly saved they must adhere to special "secret knowledge" involving restrictions of foods, normal relations in marriage, etc.

John refutes these false ideas in two ways:

1. He describes his eyewitness experience of Jesus to demonstrate that Jesus was fully God and fully man at one time.

2. He explains three ways a person can be certain of their salvation without reference to or need of any special knowledge from the Gnostic teachers.

Previously, we examined John's description of the real Jesus and the first of the ways we can be certain of our salvation. John said we can be certain by observing our behavior (he calls it walking in the light). John taught that our behavior in the areas of personal conduct (obeying the commandments), social relationships (love of the brethren), separation from the world (focus on heaven) and adherence to truth (speaking and teaching the gospel) would determine if we were walking in the light or not. It was a self-test to see if one was walking in the light (acting like a Christian) or not. If one was, it was a proof of salvation.

In this chapter we are going to look at another way we can be certain that we are saved.

Knowing the Good from the Bad — 2:28-3:10

Before we do that, however, we need to review a passage which we neglected last time. I said that the first way to assure certainty in salvation was by "walking in the light," and John explains the four ways that one behaves to prove that he is walking in the light. At the end of chapter 2 John makes a parenthetical statement about how to determine those who truly belong to Christ and those who do not. They were being seduced by false teachers and were having trouble telling the difference between the good guys and the bad guys. In 2:28-3:10 he provides them with a foolproof method.

> [28]Now, little children, abide in Him, so that when He appears, we may have confidence and not shrink away from Him in shame at His coming. [29]If you know that He is righteous, you know that everyone also who practices righteousness is born of Him.
> - I John 2:28-29

He encourages them to be faithful to Jesus so that when He returns they will not be afraid or ashamed of their unfaithfulness or sinfulness.

Then he makes the key statement that he will use in the next ten verses explaining: Everybody who does what Jesus does belongs to Jesus. In other words, the people who do what Jesus would have done, these are the good guys. These are the ones you listen to, you follow and you learn from.

> See how great a love the Father has bestowed on us, that we would be called children of God; and such we are. For this reason the world does not know us, because it did not know Him.
> - I John 3:1

John goes on to comment on how wonderful God is to make us His children (another way of saying "saved us") and because of that we are different from those in the world. So different in our conduct that we are misunderstood and sometimes persecuted in the same way that Jesus was.

> Beloved, now we are children of God, and it has not appeared as yet what we will be. We know that when He appears, we will be like Him, because we will see Him just as He is.
> - I John 3:2

He reminds them that even though there has been a change in them compared to their former lives, there will be another change when Jesus returns. We do not know exactly how we will be changed in order to exist in heaven, all we know is that we will be like Him at His appearing. The faithful who are alive at His coming will know Him and see Him when He returns, there will be no mistake (you will not miss it by accident).

> And everyone who has this hope fixed on Him
> purifies himself, just as He is pure.
> - I John 3:3

If this is so, then we are to be ready and act properly (purify ourselves, walk in the light) just as Jesus acted. Our hope is that Jesus will return and take us to heaven. Our lives and actions are based squarely on this event.

Once he has established how Christians are to act and why, he describes the very opposite conduct and what it means.

> [4]Everyone who practices sin also practices
> lawlessness; and sin is lawlessness. [5]You know
> that He appeared in order to take away sins; and in
> Him there is no sin. [6]No one who abides in Him
> sins; no one who sins has seen Him or knows Him.
> - I John 3:4-6

The key word here is "practices." The point is that those who practice (it is a habit, a way of life, a routine) a sinful lifestyle are not from God, no matter what they say. John may now be referring to that group of Gnostic teachers who advocated a hedonistic or libertine lifestyle as a way of freeing the spirit from the body. Some teachers said that since there was no connection between the soul and body, the body could do what it wanted without affecting the soul. This was a pretty attractive doctrine for those who had a weakness for worldly behavior. John tells them that Jesus died to take sinfulness away. Anyone who advocated or practiced sin was not following the one who died for sin.

> [7]Little children, make sure no one deceives you;
> the one who practices righteousness is righteous,
> just as He is righteous; [8]the one who practices sin

28

is of the devil; for the devil has sinned from the beginning. The Son of God appeared for this purpose, to destroy the works of the devil. [9]No one who is born of God practices sin, because His seed abides in him; and he cannot sin, because he is born of God. [10]By this the children of God and the children of the devil are obvious: anyone who does not practice righteousness is not of God, nor the one who does not love his brother.
- I John 3:7-10

In the final verses of this section John goes one step further by saying that not only are those who practice sin not of God, their behavior shows who they really follow: the Devil. The idea that a son of God does not sin means that a Christian does not practice or advocate sin. He tries (with various success) to practice righteousness.

Certainty by Abiding in Love — 3:11-4:21

Now that John has explained how to spot the bad guys, he gives another way that they can be certain of their salvation: love. John has already mentioned this in the discussion on walking in the light, but in this next section he amplifies and explores the true meaning of Christian love.

[11]For this is the message which you have heard from the beginning, that we should love one another; [12]not as Cain, who was of the evil one and slew his brother. And for what reason did he slay him? Because his deeds were evil, and his brother's were righteous. [13]Do not be surprised, brethren, if the world hates you.
- I John 3:11-13

Again, John reiterates the bottom line message of the gospel: love. He refers to Cain and Abel because this is the first example of the command to love being violated. He also emphasizes this central theme of Christian doctrine to show how off-center the teachings of the Gnostics were. John mentions the fact that the reason for Cain's murderous rage was his jealousy over his brother's good deeds which shone brightly alongside his own evil conduct. John says that this is also the reason behind the world's hatred of Christians (their good shows up the world's evil).

> [14]We know that we have passed out of death into life, because we love the brethren. He who does not love abides in death. [15]Everyone who hates his brother is a murderer; and you know that no murderer has eternal life abiding in him. [16]We know love by this, that He laid down His life for us; and we ought to lay down our lives for the brethren. [17]But whoever has the world's goods, and sees his brother in need and closes his heart against him, how does the love of God abide in him? [18]Little children, let us not love with word or with tongue, but in deed and truth.
> - I John 3:14-18

John emphasizes the idea that you cannot claim to be a disciple of Jesus without loving as Jesus loves. His extreme example is Jesus Himself dying to save us. In like manner we should be willing to love our brethren not in word only, but in deed as well. He repeats the idea that if you do not love or help your brethren, you do not belong to God (regardless of what you say) because you do not reflect His basic character.

> [19]We will know by this that we are of the truth, and will assure our heart before Him [20]in whatever our

> heart condemns us; for God is greater than our
> heart and knows all things. [21]Beloved, if our heart
> does not condemn us, we have confidence before
> God; [22]and whatever we ask we receive from Him,
> because we keep His commandments and do the
> things that are pleasing in His sight.
> - I John 3:19-22

A wonderful benefit and defining characteristic of those who love their brethren is that they have confidence in their salvation, a clear conscience and a powerful prayer life because the prayers of the righteous are heard and answered. The best way to dissipate guilt and fear is obeying the Lord and loving your brethren.

> [23]This is His commandment, that we believe in the
> name of His Son Jesus Christ, and love one
> another, just as He commanded us. [24]The one who
> keeps His commandments abides in Him, and He
> in him. We know by this that He abides in us, by
> the Spirit whom He has given us.
> - I John 3:23-24

They have been reduced into thinking that extreme denial of the flesh or extreme worldliness will somehow elevate them to some superior state of spiritual awareness or freedom. John explains that neither extremes will provide this. In the end, a quiet heart, peace in the face of death, confidence before God and true spirituality are the result of two basic things:

1. Faith in Jesus as the divine Savior.
2. Sincere love of the brethren who share that faith.

These two things will identify us as the ones who belong to God and possess His Spirit.

Summary

Our study has included a transitional section where John qualifies who are the good and bad: those who obey Christ are truly good, those who disobey Christ are truly bad. Note that it is not their politics, their personality or position, or what they say that determines this, it is a decision based on one's obedience to Christ. There are a lot of popular and likable people who disobey Christ so do not be fooled, John says. Those who act like Jesus are the good guys. In addition John gives another way a person can be certain that they are saved: if they love like Jesus loved and love the ones Jesus loved, they belong to God and are among the saved.

Our next chapter will be the last in John's first epistle and we will look at the final way he says we can assure ourselves of our place with God.

Reading Assignment: I John 4:1-5:21

CHAPTER 4
ABIDING IN FAITH

I JOHN 4:1-5:21

In the previous chapter we noted that John highlighted the main differences between those who were good and those who were evil, and provided a surefire test to determine who was who: the good obeyed Jesus and the evil did not. John concluded that those who loved Christ and their brethren were truly sons of God and those who didn't were not related to God even though they may have had other positive characteristics. John was doing this to reveal the hypocrisy of the false teachers who were infiltrating the church with their persuasive but false notions of true spirituality.

In effect he says to his readers, if you want to discern the truly spiritual people in the church, examine their behavior: if it conforms to the example of Christ and His teachings and especially His loving attitude, then you have a truly spiritual person. If, on the other hand, the person violates Christ's teachings and does not have love for the brethren, then this person is a fake, a son of the Devil and not a son of God. Love, according to John, is the character trait that identifies the true Christian.

At the end of chapter three the Apostle summarizes Christianity's basic doctrines:

1. Faith in Christ as Savior.

2. Love of others as an expression of that faith.

In the final chapters of this epistle John will give the third of three ways that a person can be certain that they belong to God. He will then finish with a conclusion and a summary.

Certainty by Abiding in Faith — 4:1-5:12

Let us look at our outline again to see where we are. We have seen the manner in which John describes the fully human, fully divine Jesus from his eye-witness experience. He has also explained two of the ways that Christians can be sure of their salvation (walking in the light, abiding in love). John also provides a sure method to discern the true from the false disciples and teachers (obedience to Christ, especially in the matter of loving others).

John will now finish by describing the third way that Christians can be assured of their salvation: whether or not they respect, teach and live according to Jesus' words.

[1]Beloved, do not believe every spirit, but test the spirits to see whether they are from God, because many false prophets have gone out into the world. [2]By this you know the Spirit of God: every spirit that confesses that Jesus Christ has come in the flesh is from God; [3]and every spirit that does not confess Jesus is not from God; this is the spirit of the antichrist, of which you have heard that it is coming, and now it is already in the world. [4]You are from God, little children, and have overcome them; because greater is He who is in you than he who is in the world. [5]They are from the world; therefore they speak as from the world, and the world listens to them. [6]We are from God; he who knows God

> listens to us; he who is not from God does not
> listen to us. By this we know the spirit of truth and
> the spirit of error.
> - I John 4:1-6

The word "spirit" in this section refers to teachers. In the final verses of his letter, John proceeds to deal with the false teachers head on. He offers a simple acid test for determining their legitimacy: true teachers teach that Jesus is fully human and divine. Therefore, anyone claiming spirituality, knowledge or insight will teach this teaching; those who do not, on the other hand, are not from God regardless of their personality or following. They may be sincere but they are in error.

> [7]Beloved, let us love one another, for love is from
> God; and everyone who loves is born of God and
> knows God. [8]The one who does not love does not
> know God, for God is love. [9]By this the love of God
> was manifested in us, that God has sent His only
> begotten Son into the world so that we might live
> through Him. [10]In this is love, not that we loved
> God, but that He loved us and sent His Son to be
> the propitiation for our sins. [11]Beloved, if God so
> loved us, we also ought to love one another. [12]No
> one has seen God at any time; if we love one
> another, God abides in us, and His love is
> perfected in us. [13]By this we know that we abide in
> Him and He in us, because He has given us of His
> Spirit. [14]We have seen and testify that the Father
> has sent the Son to be the Savior of the world.
> - I John 4:7-14

John repeats the idea that love is also a factor in determining the true disciple or teacher. However, he adds that God's love was the motivating factor in sending Jesus and to deny this is also to deny God's love. To neglect or change this teaching is also to neglect to teach the single most important example of God's love for man. Without Christ and proper teaching about Him we cannot attain the kind of love that sent Him and the kind of love that comes from Him. False teaching, therefore, interferes with the love that Christ has for us. John concludes that this is what they risk losing if they follow the false teachers.

> [15]Whoever confesses that Jesus is the Son of God, God abides in him, and he in God. [16]We have come to know and have believed the love which God has for us. God is love, and the one who abides in love abides in God, and God abides in him. [17]By this, love is perfected with us, so that we may have confidence in the day of judgment; because as He is, so also are we in this world. [18]There is no fear in love; but perfect love casts out fear, because fear involves punishment, and the one who fears is not perfected in love. [19]We love, because He first loved us. [20]If someone says, "I love God," and hates his brother, he is a liar; for the one who does not love his brother whom he has seen, cannot love God whom he has not seen. [21]And this commandment we have from Him, that the one who loves God should love his brother also.
> - I John 4:15-21

Again, on the same theme of love. Those who accept the proper teaching will also enjoy the fruit of that teaching in their lives which is the love of Christ in their hearts. John argues that this love will bind us to God, bind us to our brethren and fortify us against Satan's attacks. These attacks are usually meant to make us feel guilty and unsure about our salvation by accusing us of our sins and failures.

John says that we can withstand these things and have confidence and peace of mind if the love of Christ and others is in our hearts. Unsaid but inferred is that this love is only available to those who accept the teachings about the Christ as given by the Apostles. The teachings of the heretics, however, will only produce doubt, fear, pride and sorrow.

> [1]Whoever believes that Jesus is the Christ is born of God, and whoever loves the Father loves the child born of Him. [2]By this we know that we love the children of God, when we love God and observe His commandments. [3]For this is the love of God, that we keep His commandments; and His commandments are not burdensome. [4]For whatever is born of God overcomes the world; and this is the victory that has overcome the world—our faith.
> - I John 5:1-4

John repeats and builds on the idea that a good way to determine if their teachers are legitimate is to see if they abide in the faith (teach accurately the words of Christ, Matthew 28:20). This is also a good way to examine and confirm one's legitimacy as a genuine disciple thus bolstering one's confidence concerning personal salvation. John has told them that this teaching (that Jesus is the divine Savior, etc.) will produce a love for God and others. He has also emphasized the idea that false teaching will not be able to produce this fruit. Now he is trying to demonstrate how our love for God is manifested. He has already explained some of the ways that love of the brethren is shown, here he adds the important truth that obedience to Jesus' words is the way that we prove our love for God. Doing this produces three things:

1. It shows God that we love Him in the way that He wants us to demonstrate our love for Him.

2. It shows that our faith, as well as our love, are sincere and effective.

3. It shows that the world no longer owns us. We are free from the world, the flesh and the Law, once for all.

> [5]Who is the one who overcomes the world, but he who believes that Jesus is the Son of God? [6]This is the One who came by water and blood, Jesus Christ; not with the water only, but with the water and with the blood. It is the Spirit who testifies, because the Spirit is the truth. [7]For there are three that testify: [8]the Spirit and the water and the blood; and the three are in agreement. [9]If we receive the testimony of men, the testimony of God is greater; for the testimony of God is this, that He has testified concerning His Son. [10]The one who believes in the Son of God has the testimony in himself; the one who does not believe God has made Him a liar, because he has not believed in the testimony that God has given concerning His Son. [11]And the testimony is this, that God has given us eternal life, and this life is in His Son. [12]He who has the Son has the life; he who does not have the Son of God does not have the life.
> - I John 5:5-12

John offers one last challenge to the Gnostic teachers who would lure away the innocent with their promises of secret knowledge and spiritual power. He emphasizes the fact that the only way to be free from the flesh, the world (which is what the Gnostic teachers were promising), is to be free through Christ.

He reminds them of the life of Christ: the amazing witness of God at His baptism (water), the glorious ministry of His many miracles (Holy Spirit), His death and resurrection (blood). If you doubt, he says, look at the witnesses (water, Spirit, blood) that testify to the truth of what Jesus taught compared to what the false teachers are promoting. If they do not believe these witnesses and the promise of eternal life that these witnesses have made, they then forfeit the promise. And make no mistake, he says, the promise of eternal life is only offered through Christ and His teachings, not through the secret and false teachings of these Gnostic teachers. His argument to them is that they should not simply listen to him, but rather listen to the witnesses.

Summary — 5:13-21

In the final verses John will summarize and close his letter concerning this subject.

> [13]These things I have written to you who believe in the name of the Son of God, so that you may know that you have eternal life. [14]This is the confidence which we have before Him, that, if we ask anything according to His will, He hears us. [15]And if we know that He hears us in whatever we ask, we know that we have the requests which we have asked from Him.
> - I John 5:13-15

This letter ends in much the same way that John's gospel ends. He could write much more and continue the argument but these three ways of assuring salvation (walking in the light, love, faith) and how to discern true from false teachers should be enough to preserve and strengthen their faith. His encouragement is that if they pray to God for help to do these things, He will answer their prayers.

> ^{16}If anyone sees his brother committing a sin not leading to death, he shall ask and God will for him give life to those who commit sin not leading to death. There is a sin leading to death; I do not say that he should make request for this. ^{17}All unrighteousness is sin, and there is a sin not leading to death.
> - I John 5:16-17

Jesus talked about the sin that leads to death in Mark 3:29 and Luke 12:10, *"And everyone who speaks a word against the Son of Man, it will be forgiven him; but he who blasphemes against the Holy Spirit, it will not be forgiven him."*

In context Jesus was referring to those who were saying that He was of the Devil and His teachings were false. John has been talking about people who claim Jesus is a ghost and His teachings are not inspired or are incomplete. I believe John is echoing Jesus here by saying that all manner of sin is forgivable except denying Christ, denying His word or denying His work. This is blaspheming of the Holy Spirit because He is the One who brings Christ, His word and His cross to the world. The point being made is that if you deny these things then there is nowhere else to go for forgiveness. John says you can pray that God forgive men's weaknesses, immoralities, irreverence and failures, but do not ask Him to forgive those who promote false teachings or rejection of Christ because there is no other way for them to be saved.

He finishes with four things all Christians should know:

> We know that no one who is born of God sins; but He who was born of God keeps him, and the evil one does not touch him.
> - I John 5:18

40

1. Christians are not slaves of sin. The cross cleanses us and the Holy Spirit empowers us to be free from the slavery of habitual sin.

> We know that we are of God, and that the whole world lies in the power of the evil one.
> - I John 5:19

2. Christians know that there are only two kingdoms in this world: the kingdom of God and the kingdom of Satan. You are in one or the other since there is no neutral place.

> And we know that the Son of God has come, and has given us understanding so that we may know Him who is true; and we are in Him who is true, in His Son Jesus Christ. This is the true God and eternal life.
> - I John 5:20

3. Christians know and proclaim that Jesus Christ is the Son of God and Savior. Those who are with Him are saved and those who are not are not saved.

> Little children, guard yourselves from idols.
> - I John 5:21

4. Worshiping any other God or form of God is wrong and not a part of Christian teaching. Beware of those who try to make it so.

John ends with a warning to his flock and a warning to those who would seduce them to follow after the vain idols of human philosophy or speculation rather than the gospel message preached by the Apostles. The same kinds of attacks against Christians are made today in the guise of various philosophies like evolution or humanism, etc. These and all other attempts to explain life and death without Christ are in the spirit of what John refers to as the Antichrist.

Reading Assignment: II John

CHAPTER 5
JOHN'S
COVER LETTER

II JOHN

John's first epistle dealt with the problem of Gnosticism in the early church. As mentioned before, Gnosticism comes from the word "gnosis" which means knowledge. In the case of this teaching, however, it refers to occult or secret knowledge possessed by the Gnostic teachers. The Gnostics taught that we are souls trapped in a prison-like material world by an evil divinity. We are kept unaware of our plight by the carnal seductions of this world, and only those with the secret knowledge (gnosis) of the true state of affairs can transcend this prison and enter a higher reality. They also taught that the "good" divinity dwelling above this evil realm aided lost souls by sending a messenger of truth to reveal this deception (*Note that this is roughly the plot line for the 1999 movie The Matrix with Keanu Reeves as "the one"/Jesus*).

It was easy, therefore, to superimpose this teaching onto the gospel and make Jesus the messenger of truth, and they, the Gnostic teachers, the guardians of the secret knowledge. There was only one problem with this: Jesus claimed that He was God and inhabited a human body. Jesus also taught that the truth made one free (John 8:32), revealed that all were prisoners of their own sinfulness, and freedom from guilt and condemnation was accomplished through His ministry on the cross and received by faith, not secret knowledge. As a matter of fact, He commanded that this good news be shared with the entire world and not be kept secret. Jesus empowered every soul to find salvation from sin, not just those who had the secret. He also taught that material things had no power to defile us; the material world was created by God who ruled over it and that it was a good thing, *"God saw all that He had made, and behold, it was very good (Genesis 1:31)."*

Like many heretics, the Gnostic teachers tried to merge their teachings with the gospel. They denied that Jesus was actually God and said that He was an apparition of God, or that He became human only at the cross, but not that He was God and man simultaneously. They mixed in certain Jewish traditions and food laws, and taught that to be free from the evil corruption of this material prison you had to practice asceticism (denial of the flesh). Some, however, taught the opposite: that since the soul was separate from the flesh, whatever one did in the flesh had no affect on the soul. These teachings led those who accepted them to either practice a severe type of legalism or fall into a life of hedonistic dissipation. Such was the effect on the church by these teachers in creating confusion and doubt among the believers.

John writes a letter in response to these men and their influence. He begins with his eyewitness account of Jesus, the Jesus who did and said things only a divine being could say and do; the Jesus that John actually saw, heard and touched in human form and thus established his witness concerning Jesus' dual nature.

In the first epistle, we reviewed how John encouraged his readers to be confident of their salvation without the special knowledge or practice of the false teachers. He wrote that there were three ways to be certain:

1. Certainty by walking in the light. They knew they were saved because they lived and acted like saved people.

2. Certainty by abiding in love. They knew they were saved because they acted out of love in every situation.

3. Certainty by abiding in faith. They knew they were saved because they believed and relied on Jesus, not secret man-made knowledge.

John's gospel told the story of Jesus' incarnation and sacrifice on the cross. John's first epistle encouraged his readers to believe that information. The two (gospel and epistle) worked together to tell them that they left their "flesh" not through secret knowledge, but through faith in Jesus Christ based on their knowledge of and belief in Him.

The Second Epistle of John

This letter is shorter than I John and covers much of the same material. What is interesting is how the letter was used. II John is not a continuation of John's gospel or his first epistle, it is a cover letter that accompanied the epistle and gospel. It was written to a specific church with the intention of warning it about the things which John spoke of in the first letter. The main point of the letter was to warn the church of the great danger posed by the false teachers and their teachings. John says that they needed to be vigilant.

Outline — II John

Text — II John

Salutation - Verses 1-3

> [1]The elder to the chosen lady and her children, whom I love in truth; and not only I, but also all who know the truth, [2]for the sake of the truth which abides in us and will be with us forever:
> - II John 1:1-2

John is the elder (he was old and a leader in the church at Ephesus at this time). The chosen lady and her children are the church. He writes this to a particular congregation. He uses euphemisms because of the danger of persecution by the Roman government. He says that he loves this church as does all those who hold to the truth. The truth is the gospel and in this case the essential truth of the gospel (that Jesus is the divine Son of God and Savior). He tells them that all those who love this truth are loved by John and by one another. It is this truth that binds all Christians together in love forever.

> Grace, mercy and peace will be with us, from God
> the Father and from Jesus Christ, the Son of the
> Father, in truth and love.
> - II John 1:3

He pronounces a blessing from God and places the source
of the divine blessing equally at the feet of both God the
Father and Jesus Christ. John knows that there is some
confusion among them about who Jesus really is and thus
settles the matter at the outset by referring to Jesus as One
having an equal and similar nature as God. He asks for three
things that only God can offer:

1. **Grace**: In this case, a favor to avoid punishment from
   sin.

2. **Mercy**: Compassion for human weaknesses and
   failures.

3. **Peace**: No war or judgment because of sin, but rather
   peace between ourselves and our judge who is God.

John asks these blessings on the people from both God and
Jesus thus securing a blessing for his readers but also re-
emphasizing the exalted position of Jesus Christ, far above
the one given to Him by the false teachers.

Commendation — Verses 4-6

> I was very glad to find some of your children
> walking in truth, just as we have received
> commandment to do from the Father.
> - II John 1:4

In contrast to those Christians who have been deceived or those who are doing the deceiving with their false teaching, John commends those who are living according to the truth concerning Jesus Christ. Once again, he connects the teaching and revelation concerning the gospel of Jesus to the Father, as opposed to the human concepts being proposed by the Gnostic teachers.

> Now I ask you, lady, not as though I were writing to you a new commandment, but the one which we have had from the beginning, that we love one another.
> - II John 1:5

Their proper understanding of who Jesus really is will be reflected in their lifestyle. The distinguishing lifestyle of one who truly understands the gospel and accepts Jesus as divine Lord is love, because this is the lifestyle that He Himself modeled.

> And this is love, that we walk according to His commandments. This is the commandment, just as you have heard from the beginning, that you should walk in it.
> - II John 1:6

John merely summarizes the entire life and teaching of Christ in one word: love. If you love God and Christ you will love others, self and obey Christ's commands. He commends those who have believed correctly and have acted correctly based on that belief.

Warning — Verses 7-11

Now that he has spoken to the Christians who have stood fast in doctrine and practice, he turns his attention to those who are being swayed by the false teachers.

> For many deceivers have gone out into the world, those who do not acknowledge Jesus Christ as coming in the flesh. This is the deceiver and the antichrist.
> - II John 1:7

He denounces the false teachers by first describing the essence of their incorrect doctrine (that Jesus was not fully human, just a spirit). He accuses them of being deceivers, not simply making an innocent mistake or having a lack of understanding concerning their doctrine, but men purposefully deceiving the church with their teachings. He charges them with being pawns of the Antichrist, that force which exists in the world under many guises with the purpose of defeating the gospel of Christ and His church. Jesus spoke of "false Christs and false prophets" who would come into the world with the purpose of deceiving the saints in the very name of Jesus (Matthew 24:23-24).

> [8]Watch yourselves, that you do not lose what we have accomplished, but that you may receive a full reward. [9]Anyone who goes too far and does not abide in the teaching of Christ, does not have God; the one who abides in the teaching, he has both the Father and the Son.
> - II John 1:8-9

His warning is couched in terms of what you gain or lose by being careful not to be deceived. If you remain faithful to the gospel and Christ then you keep your reward (eternal life) and your relationship with the Father and Son. If, on the other hand, you fall away from the teaching then you risk your reward and your relationship.

This is a good answer to those who claim that doctrine is not really that important or essential. John warns them that to have the wrong doctrine and practice of Christianity can lead to loss of faith and, consequently, loss of reward.

> [10]If anyone comes to you and does not bring this teaching, do not receive him into your house, and do not give him a greeting; [11]for the one who gives him a greeting participates in his evil deeds.
> - II John 1:10-11

John adds a practical way to implement his warning. In those days the offering of hospitality to strangers was an important social practice, especially for Christians. It was a sign of Christian love, faith and maturity. However, it was also a way of providing support for preachers and teachers in the church who travelled from place to place ministering to different churches. John says that one was not bound to offer hospitality, even to a teacher or preacher, if that person did not maintain the proper teaching of the gospel. He tells them, on the contrary, to discourage such a one by denying him hospitality and not even to greet him.

This seems harsh, but understand that the false teachers were sowing the seeds of a soul's destruction with their doctrines. They had to be stopped. John warns the brethren not to allow false teachers the opportunity to set up a base for teaching others in their homes (how teachers of that day operated, even the Apostles - Matthew 10:11). He concludes by saying that even to offer the usual greeting (the hope that all is well or that God will bless their efforts) was not to be given less they offer any type of encouragement to these people. This is why I feel no guilt in refusing money to religious causes who do not honor Jesus as Lord, nor do I allow any group or person into my home to teach or promote an idea that disclaims the position of Christ (e.g. Jehovah's Witnesses - Jesus is a spirit or angel).

Conclusion — Verses 12-13

> [12]Though I have many things to write to you, I do not want to do so with paper and ink; but I hope to come to you and speak face to face, so that your joy may be made full. [13]The children of your chosen sister greet you.
> - II John 1:12-13

John ends on a personal note that is more fully explained in his third letter. The problem in general, the issue of false teachers and how to respond to them, has been addressed. A more personal problem exists in this church involving certain individuals so John says he would rather deal with these issues in person, not in writing. He closes with a final greeting from the church where he is based (Ephesus). We do not know which particular congregation he is writing to.

Lessons

1. Doctrine is Important
Incorrect teaching and understanding can cause us to lose our salvation. It is important for elders, teachers and preachers to be on guard at all times (they are to correct and reprove those who teach or promote false ideas - Romans 16:17).

2. Doctrine Guides Actions

What you do is based largely on what you believe. Many who do not act like Christians usually lack proper teaching and understanding. These need to be corrected using God's word appropriately.

3. Doctrine Decides Discipleship

There are many "nice" people who reject Jesus. You can have a relationship with a friend or family member who is not a Christian, but the one thing you can't have with those who do not believe is Christian fellowship.

Reading Assignment: III John

CHAPTER 6
LIFE IN THE EARLY CHURCH

III JOHN

This is our final study on the epistles of the Apostle John. The first two of his three letters were mainly a defense of Christian doctrine against a type of Gnosticism that attempted to merge Greek philosophical ideas with the Christian gospel. This caused both discouragement and division in the church, and John wrote his first two epistles to address these false teachings warning the heretic teachers and reassuring the church as to the content, power and result of the true gospel in the life of every believer.

An interesting feature of this third letter is that aside from its teaching content, the epistle also provides a glimpse into the workings of the first century church. It seems that at that time much of the ministry was carried out by itinerant or traveling preachers who would go from one congregation to another preaching and teaching as they went. In each place they would preach publicly and hold meetings in the homes where they were staying as guests. There was always the danger of abuse in this system because false teachers and swindlers could easily take advantage of the kind and trusting people who were providing them with hospitality. In this environment, hospitality was a very important element in the life and growth of the church. It was risky, but necessary.

John's third letter mentions three men in the church, one who welcomed these traveling missionaries, one who did not and one who was in need of this hospitality. Gaius was a brother who supported and fed the traveling preachers, Diotrephes would not receive or allow them to preach, and Demetrius was one who needed the hospitality as possibly a missionary sent by John. In his letter John commends Gaius, and warns Diotriphes of a test of authority when he (John) would come to visit in person. He also commends Demetrius to the church. This situation was about power and its use in the assembly, and how one man was exerting his authority to maintain power and control.

With this in mind, here is a possible outline for this epistle that can help us follow John's thinking as we review his letter line by line.

Outline and Text — III John

Introduction — Verse 1

> The elder to the beloved Gaius, whom I love in
> truth.
> - III John 1:1

John does not name himself because the recipient knows him and is aware of his position and role. He also uses the same introduction as II John. His use of the term "elder" suggests that by this time he was known as the last surviving Apostle, advanced in years, filled with wisdom and the Spirit. It was a reference to him alone as the "elder." In other cases where church leaders were concerned the reference was always to the "elders."

John's connection to Gaius is the same as his bond with all the others, he loves him in connection with the truth. The truth is the gospel and all that the gospel produces in a person. His love for Gaius, therefore, has been produced by the truth in him and motivated by the fact that Gaius shares with John and others the knowledge and belief in this truth. The elder/Apostle loves Gaius in this manner (agape type love) because he is a faithful brother in the Lord.

Blessing — Verses 2-4

> Beloved, I pray that in all respects you may prosper and be in good health, just as your soul prospers.
> - III John 1:2

John says that his prayers are for Gaius' material and physical well-being as well as his spiritual progress. A complete blessing considers all facets of life: material, physical and spiritual. In essence, John prays for Gaius to have a balanced life enriched in every area.

> For I was very glad when brethren came and testified to your truth, that is, how you are walking in truth.
> - III John 1:3

John is happy to offer this prayer, and it is almost reflexive because the news on Gaius is that he continues to be faithful to the gospel/truth. Walking in truth means that one lives by the revelation of the gospel and its teachings. We think that responding to the gospel is a one time act (believe, repent, confess, baptize). But walking in truth means that this cycle of response is an ongoing exercise that becomes the substance of our daily life of faith.

For example, I continually grow in my knowledge of and belief in the word of God as well as its proper application in my life. I am constantly challenged by the Holy Spirit about my ways, and I renew my efforts at repenting and discarding worldly, sinful conduct for the true and right way to live and think shown to me in God's word. I grow bolder and more adept at confessing Jesus Christ with my life, my words, my service, my giving and my sacrifice. When I first did this (confess my faith in Jesus before being baptized), it was a cold November night in front of two people. Since then I have confessed Christ before millions of people through my effort to teach and preach using various media (newspapers, radio, TV, Internet, books, etc.). I constantly make the effort to bury my pride, my will, my "self" in the baptism of humility in order to be daily resurrected to a greater likeness of Christ.

John sees in Gaius a man who is walking or living in this ongoing truth and he loves to see this in him, it becomes an extension of his love for Christ.

> I have no greater joy than this, to hear of my
> children walking in the truth.
> - III John 1:4

As a matter of fact, to see this phenomenon take place in any member of the church causes John the greatest joy. Observing the transformation of another into a more Christ-like image is a very gratifying experience, especially if you have helped nurture that person's faith.

Encouraging Workers for Truth
— Verses 5-8

> [5]Beloved, you are acting faithfully in whatever you accomplish for the brethren, and especially when they are strangers; [6]and they have testified to your love before the church. You will do well to send them on their way in a manner worthy of God.
> - III John 1:5-6

John commends the work that Gaius and others are doing in providing hospitality for the evangelists and missionaries that are coming their way. Hospitality comes from a Greek word which means "the love of strangers." To offer food and lodging to strangers was not only an act of faith, it was also a great help in spreading the gospel. John and the church in Ephesus heard reports that Gaius treated the missionaries sent his way in a generous manner. He commends and encourages him to not only continue offering this hospitality but also urges Gaius to provide supplies and resources for their journey after they leave his home.

> [7]For they went out for the sake of the Name, accepting nothing from the Gentiles. [8]Therefore we ought to support such men, so that we may be fellow workers with the truth.
> - III John 1:7-8

Concerning these missionaries, John says that their sole motivation was their faith in Christ (the Name) and they did not solicit or accept any payment from those they preached to (the Gentiles). This dedication and integrity needed to be supported by the believers. After all, if the believers did not support the missionaries, who would? Even though Gaius was not the one teaching and preaching the word, his efforts at providing hospitality was his participation and contribution to the overall evangelistic effort which was acceptable to God.

We cannot all be in the mission field, we do not all have the ability to be effective personal workers, but to the extent that we support and assist this work, we share in both the ministry and the rewards that come from it.

Reproving the Opponents of Truth — Verses 9-11

> I wrote something to the church; but Diotrephes, who loves to be first among them, does not accept what we say.
> - III John 1:9

John focuses on the issue that prompted the writing of this letter. He has sent a previous letter in which, some scholars think, he gave the church instructions to receive certain missionaries and which Diotrephes refused to make public or honor. Others believe that he is referring to his second epistle. Whichever case it was, Diotrephes was blocking communication between John and the church in an attempt to challenge John's authority as an Apostle and teacher.

> For this reason, if I come, I will call attention to his deeds which he does, unjustly accusing us with wicked words; and not satisfied with this, he himself does not receive the brethren, either, and he forbids those who desire to do so and puts them out of the church.
> - III John 1:10

John now reviews the unacceptable and sinful behavior of Diotrephes. These include:

- Unjust accusations against John and other leaders.
- Unwillingness to receive teachers and missionaries sent there.
- Interference with those who tried to offer hospitality.
- Creating division by putting out of the church those who opposed him.

This man wanted the power of leadership and tried to undermine John's authority as an Apostle and those who responded to John in order to get it. This is an old pattern used even to this day. Some desire power and authority in the church or refuse to follow the leadership in place, so they begin a quiet (and sometimes not so quiet) campaign of criticism, negative commentary and slander against those who have leadership roles.

John says that he will deal with this person by exposing the light of truth on his sins and misdeeds. There will be no fistfight, no political intrigue, no debate or contest to see who is better, stronger or smarter. John will demonstrate the other man's weaknesses by comparing his actions and attitudes to the Word of truth. Let the gospel be the judge, then the truth will come out and everyone will be able to see clearly and thus decide.

> Beloved, do not imitate what is evil, but what is good. The one who does good is of God; the one who does evil has not seen God.
> - III John 1:11

John reminds Gaius and the church to not be influenced by what this person is doing. It is tempting to fight fire with fire, evil with evil, power with greater power. However, this is the kingdom of God, not the world. Things operate differently here. John encourages them to imitate the things that have been taught which are good in order to counter the creeping evil that is making its way into the church. It is not good to succumb to pride and selfish ambition. However, it is good to offer hospitality to the missionaries, and good to face evil men by revealing their sins and not sharing in them.

John tells them that those who act in this way prove that they have seen (recognized) Jesus as God, and those who do not act in this way neither know the truth nor have seen (recognized) that Jesus truly is God, and not just another teacher.

Commending the Witness of Truth

> Demetrius has received a good testimony from everyone, and from the truth itself; and we add our testimony, and you know that our testimony is true.
> - III John 1:12

John gives a commendation concerning Demetrius, the teacher/missionary being sent who may be at the center of this conflict. The Apostle gives three references:

1. The church commends him.

2. The truth commends him (meaning that he preaches the truth and lives in accordance to his preaching).

3. The elder, John himself, vouches for his character and works.

This should be enough to recommend someone and overcome any doubts or questions anyone has, including Diotrephes.

Conclusion — Verses 13-15

> [13]I had many things to write to you, but I am not willing to write them to you with pen and ink; [14]but I hope to see you shortly, and we will speak face to face. [15]Peace be to you. The friends greet you. Greet the friends by name.
> - III John 1:13-15

John finishes the letter with some personal notes on various points. He has formulated many things to say to Gaius but decides not to write them, preferring to speak with him face to face. He is sending the letter ahead of his visit to prepare the way. He plans to go there in person shortly after the letter arrives. This he will do without warning in order to deal with Diotriphes and not give him a chance to stir up trouble in advance.

He offers the blessing that these brothers need: peace. He greets the many mutual acquaintances that he and Gaius share. He ends on this positive, personal and forward-looking note.

Summary / Lessons

There are several lessons that we can draw from this very brief, very personal letter from John to his Christian friend Gaius concerning the problem of powerful men trying to dominate the church.

1. Teaching the Truth is Important

John commends them for knowing and living according to the truth. What they say, do, think, how they worship, what they preach and teach, are all done according to what is true. This is another way of saying, "according to God's word," because Jesus says that it is God's word that is true (John 17:7). This is only possible because they have learned the truth from someone who taught them (in this case it may have been John himself).

My point here is that in order to live according to the truth one must be taught that truth. The task of knowing, teaching and passing that truth along from generation to generation belongs to the church (I Timothy 3:15), and within the church that task falls to every teacher, preacher and ultimately every elder. From the nursery class to adult Bible classes, it is important that we are very careful to always teach the truth from God's word and not substitute this for human ideas (no matter how noble). We cannot live according to the truth and thus be pleasing to God unless we are constantly being taught the truth by those responsible for this ministry.

2. Those who Teach the Truth Deserve our Support

There are usually dozens of people involved in a church's education program. Those include elders, ministers, deacons, teachers, coordinators and assistants. All of these saints deserve our support. Some make a living at it and deserve what they receive, others volunteer and deserve our gratitude. All of these, however, deserve the church's cooperation in getting kids to class, maintaining their own presence and encouraging these people's efforts to teach the truth. We will buy an overpriced souvenir to support our sports hero and film stars but often neglect to say thank you to those who are leading our souls to heaven.

3. Those who Teach the Truth must also Live by the Truth

Diotrephes may have denied hospitality and caused problems in the church out of a warped sense of duty to protect or defend a truth that only he saw. His actions, however, were contrary to the truth given by the Apostles and received by the church. Demetrius, on the other hand, received affirmation because his actions coincided with the truth he had received from the Apostles. It is not difficult to spot the fakes, either their words do not match the words of Jesus, or their actions do not match their words. Remember that those who aspire to teach have the dual responsibility of teaching only what is true and living according to that truth.

4. Hospitality is Still an Important and Necessary Ministry

We don't rely on hospitality today to take care of our missionaries and evangelists, however, hospitality is still crucial in the development of a New Testament church. If we are not sharing our homes, not making strangers feel welcome, not helping new families feel part of our church family, we are neglecting a primary mission and ministry of the church: hospitality. Hospitality is inconvenient, expensive and time consuming, but this is what makes it so pleasing to God. When we offer hospitality we are truly giving of ourselves and that is what makes it special and worthy of being offered to the Lord.

BibleTalk.tv is an Internet Mission Work.

We provide textual Bible teaching material on our website and mobile apps for free. We enable churches and individuals all over the world to have access to high quality Bible materials for personal growth, group study or for teaching in their classes.

The goal of this mission work is to spread the gospel to the greatest number of people using the latest technology available. For the first time in history it is becoming possible to preach the gospel to the entire world at once. BibleTalk.tv is an effort to preach the gospel to all nations every day until Jesus returns.

The Choctaw Church of Christ in Oklahoma City is the sponsoring congregation for this work and provides the oversight for the BibleTalk ministry team. If you would like information on how you can support this ministry, please go to the link provided below.

bibletalk.tv/support

Made in the USA
Monee, IL
23 May 2023